ELDEST DAUGHTER

For Valerie –
and our long friendship
and mutual growth –
Love
Ava

ELDEST DAUGHTER

poems

AVA LEAVELL HAYMON

LOUISIANA STATE UNIVERSITY PRESS BATON ROUGE

Published by Louisiana State University Press

Manufactured in the United States of America
FIRST PRINTING

DESIGNER: *Mandy McDonald Scallan*
TYPEFACE: *Calluna*
PRINTER: *McNaughton & Gunn, Inc.*
BINDER: *Dekker Bookbinding*

Library of Congress Cataloging-in-Publication Data
Haymon, Ava Leavell.
[Poems. Selections]
Eldest daughter : poems / Ava Leavell Haymon.
pages cm
ISBN 978-0-8071-5336-9 (cloth : alk. paper) — ISBN 978-0-8071-5337-6 (pbk. : alk. paper) — ISBN 978-0-8071-5338-3 (pdf) — ISBN 978-0-8071-5339-0 (epub) — ISBN 978-0-8071-5340-6 (mobi)
I. Title.
PS3608.A945A6 2013
811'.6—dc23

2013011599

The paper in this book meets the guidelines for permanence and durability of the Committee on Production Guidelines for Book Longevity of the Council on Library Resources. ∞

for my father
who taught me
the two sides of the human heart

Somewhere, out beyond ideas
of wrongdoing and right-doing,
there is a field.

I will meet you there.

—RUMI

CONTENTS

Acknowledgments | xi

Preacher's Daughter

In Gratitude for a Southern Baptist Upbringing | 3

"Louie's: Home of the Veggie Omelet" | 5

Eva/Ave at the National Gallery | 7

In Which I Forgive My Mother Her Intentions | 9

Preacher's Daughter | 11

Contralto Recitative with Angel Chorus | 15

The Holy Ghost Develops Binge/Purge Syndrome | 17

The Holy Ghost Attends Vacation Bible School | 18

The Holy Ghost Tries Out for Little League | 19

The Holy Ghost Moves to Kilgore | 20

Church Schism: Every Body's Got to Be Some Place | 21

Four-Year-Old Invents a New Curse Word | 22

The Holy Ghost Designs the Perfect Woman | 24

Why the Groundhog Fears Her Shadow

Changing Weather Patterns | 29

Shining | 30
The Center Cannot | 32
She Begins with the Sky | 34
The Child Born | 35
The Dream Runs On | 36
Color of the Moon | 38
The Heads of Old Dolls | 39
Groundhog's Prayer of Petition | 40
Why the Groundhog Fears Her Shadow | 41
How Two Became One Again: Sestinas' Work Done | 43
Winter's End | 45
Staying at the Willard | 46
Parish Courthouse, Cameron | 49
Woman in the Middle | 50

The Castle of Either/Or: a fairy tale
The Castle of Either/Or | 53

Daughter's Fealty
Continental Divide | 61
Steam Calliope | 63
Bass Fishing with a Hulapopper | 68
Roundball | 75
"My Father Will Have Two Dozen on the Halfshell" | 80

Notes | 81

ACKNOWLEDGMENTS

Anthologies

From Dusk to Need: 25 Years of Flume Press Chapbooks, edited by Casey Huff (Chico, CA: Flume Press, 2010): “Four-Year-Old Invents a New Curse Word” (there titled “Godshit”), “In Gratitude for a Southern Baptist Upbringing,” and “In Which I Forgive My Mother Her Intentions”; *Improbable Worlds, an Anthology of Texas and Louisiana Poets,* edited by Martha Sherpas (Houston: Mutabilis Press, 2012): “The Heads of Old Dolls”; *National Poetry Competition Winners Anthology* (Chardon, OH: Chester H. Jones Foundation, 1987); “‘My Father Will Have Two Dozen on the Halfshell’”; *Rape, Incest, Battery,* edited by Miriam Kalman Harris (New York: Perseus Publishing, 2003): “Why the Groundhog Fears Her Shadow” (there titled “In Which, on the Fourth Anniversary of His Death”); *Turnings: Writing on Women's Transformations,* edited by Luisa Igloria and Renee Olander (Norfolk, VA: Friends of Women's Studies at Old Dominion University, 2000): “Parish Courthouse, Cameron”; *Uncommonplace: An Anthology of Contemporary Louisiana Poets,* edited by Ann Brewster Dobie (Baton Rouge: Louisiana State University Press, 1998): “The Holy Ghost Goes Out for Little League” (there “The Holy Ghost Goes Out for Little League”).

Chapbooks

Many poems appeared in these chapbooks after journal publication. Some appeared in these for the first time, and these are noted here. My deep thanks to the editors and presses that published these chapbooks. Their encouragement and comments have been invaluable.

Built in Fear of Heat (winner of Nightshade Press national chapbook competition; San Francisco: Nightshade Press, 1994); *Kitchen Heat* (Houston: Maude's Head Press, 1991; chapbook with the same title as full collection, which was published by LSU Press in 2006); *Staving Off Rapture* (winner of the Flume Press national chapbook competition; Chico, CA: Flume Press, 1994): "Contralto Recitative" and "The Holy Ghost Designs the Perfect Woman"; *Why the Groundhog Fears Her Shadow* (Greensboro, NC: March Street Press, 1995): Continental Divide" (there titled "Loveland Pass"), "Eva/Ave at the National Gallery," and "Shining" (there titled "Disclosure").

Journals

My profound gratitude to the journals in which these poems first appeared, many in earlier versions or with different titles. The comments and encouragement from the editors have been invaluable to me.

Cooweescoowee: "Bass Fishing With a Hulapopper"; *The Georgia Review:* "In Which I Forgive My Mother Her Intentions" (anthologized, see above); *Image:* "Changing Weather Patterns" (there titled "Advent"); *Lip Service:* "The Dream Runs On" (there titled "Favorite Patient Lets the Dream Run On"); *Louisiana English Journal:* "Staying at the Willard" and "Why the Groundhog Fears Her Shadow" (anthologized, see above); *Louisiana Literature:* "Roundball"; *Mildred:* "The Child Born"; *New Delta Review:* "The Holy Ghost Attends Vacation Bible School" and "The Holy Ghost Moves to Kilgore" (both Pushcart Prize nominations); *The New Orleans Review:* "The Heads of Old Dolls"; *Northwest Review:* "In Gratitude for a Southern Baptist Upbringing" (there titled "Sestina in Gratitude for a Southern Baptist Upbringing," also anthologized twice, see list above); *Open 24 hrs:* "Four-Year-Old Invents a New Curse Word" (there titled "Godshit," anthologized, see above); *Oxford Magazine:* "The Holy Ghost Develops Binge/

Purge Syndrome" (there titled "Bulimia"); *Rose & Thorn:* "The Castle of Either/Or," "The Center Cannot," "How to Become One Again," "Winter's End," and "Woman in the Middle"; *Shenandoah:* "The Holy Ghost Tries Out for Little League" (there titled "The Holy Ghost Goes Out for Little League"); *Swamp Lily:* "Groundhog's Prayer of Petition" (anthologized, see above), "My Father Will Have Three Dozen on the Halfshell," and "Parish Courthouse, Cameron" (anthologized, see above); *Talking River:* "She Must Begin with the Sky" (there titled "One Always Must Begin with the Sky"); *The Taos Review:* "'Louie's: Home of the Veggie; Omelet'"; *Turnrow:* "Name the Color of the Moon" (anthologized, see above); *Zone 3:* "The Holy Ghost in a Church Schism."

Videos

MADstudio: *Protect Your Domain Name,* Michael Daugherty, Steven David Beck, and Ava Leavell Haymon. Section II, in "Preacher's Daughter," used in video as poem/text and voice-over titled in the video "Bereshit (In the Beginning)."

PREACHER'S DAUGHTER

We continually explore for the invisible
power structure behind the visible kings.

—BUCKMINSTER FULLER

. . . my steady partner is going to be mystery.

—NANCY DREW

In Gratitude for a Southern Baptist Upbringing

My father, his father, all the family men preached sin
as though proclaiming the word often enough
from the pulpit would wrestle it out of our hearts.
Every Sunday a new sin, usually something about sex
and usually committed by a woman.
They all had those heavy cannon voices,

and it's the King James roll of those baritone voices,
seminary-trained, huge without microphones, that made sin
sound so sensual to me, a child-woman
suffering through puberty, suffering sermons enough
to leave me no time to dabble into sex
on my own, when the wish did nibble its way into my heart.

And there's no question it was our hearts
they were after, those masculine voices
—sure as brass horns—trumpeting sex
even while they railed against sin.
But no conversion, no confession was quite enough
to earn me praise—as virtuous woman,

virgin without stain, price-above-rubies, a woman
who could ponder things in her heart
the way Mary did. It was never enough—
my modesty, my soprano solos, coloraturo little voice
from the wrong side of the family. A sin,
the girlish register, a range of high notes that shimmered sex

just when I yearned—so earnest!—to stifle sex
and anything else that branded me woman,
adulteress, harlot, vessel of sin
who tempted righteous Adam, soul and heart,
in that seductive bel canto voice
sticky with cinnamon and apples. Enough

that I looked like her, Eve. Enough
that my newly furred sex
was hers. My name, Ava. My voice,
the Delilah tones of a woman,
the one with flesh heart
who first embraced sin.

I'd heard so much about sin in church, I knew enough
to go at it whole heart, when the time came for sex.
I'm glad to be woman, brought up right:
to sing desire in my own voice.

"Louie's: Home of the Veggie Omelet"

on the cook's t-shirt

Louie's at eleven,
waiting for Mona Lisa.
The cook saws

a frozen muffin in two
and sticks it in the toaster.
I ask for some tea and squeeze

the bag. The place
fills up, it's getting noisy.
Mona Lisa must have forgotten.

Arms wave along the counter,
stories warm, inflate. The cook
moves faster, beats eggs

with a fork. Chamomile tea,
hot down my throat. I open
in two halves, like the waffle iron—

head to toe, along a cleft
parallel to my nose, an altarpiece
carving of God

the Father, that creaks open
on its medieval hinges
to the Mary and baby

nesting inside. Her forehead
is grave, Flemish. She is
handing the baby the round ball

of the world. I go ahead and order:
veggie omelet, toast
with no butter, refill,

same tea bag. The gold leaf
of the ball is dimmed
with age, Mary's blue gone

to patches of indigo and worm-
riddled wood. I'm going to eat
alone: She's forgotten,

I'm sure of it. The griddle
goes yellow with my egg.
The gold ball's

not the sun, not the earth—the baby
cracks it with one hand.
A yellow blanket wraps

bean sprouts, bell pepper,
chopped zucchini, celery,
red cabbage, onion.

Eva/Ave at the National Gallery

Flemish Virgin with a severe underbite
and receding chin—grinds her teeth
at night, I'll bet. The show is *Eva/Ave:*
Images of Woman in the Renaissance and Baroque,
the Mother of God is dying for the 10th time
in this room alone, and here #41 Anonymous German
Fifteenth Century, School of Peter Maler,
finally gets it right. Maria, Ave, handmaiden,
hand-colored, the green's faded almost tan,
the carmine to dull pink, gouged
outlines harsh and black as ever.

Poor Ave, not yet assumed,
not overarched by sketchy graven angels
like the big Rembrandt to the left,
not rolling her eyes up in ecstasy
out of fleshy cheeks as does her analog
after Peter Paul Rubens down the way.
Just dying, the way everyone does, or will.
Her mouth slants down. A halo, clunky
as a Kennedy half dollar, bumps
her head off the pillow.

She's got the best room in the catalogue—
the Eves and their Snakes petered out
2 rooms ago—but the famous face wads
into bitterness. No gratitude at being cast
the virgin, not the whore. No show
of courage for the . . . 12 men! Poor Ave!
I count them more than once.

They range around the Dutch Interior bed.
Wavy letters spell their names like cartoon odors.
Johans, Peter, Phillipp. Each turns a flat eye
to his hagiography, every man for himself.
Their halos, solid disks with no light,
overlap back, front, back, front.

What a way to die. She's had to keep
her wimple tied. No woman there
to rub her wrist or fold a warm cloth
between her legs. A mandorla, possibly
added later, floats on the background—
a young girl with a baby who pulls away.

Which is worse for her, to stay or go?
Endure earth with these ecclesiastic nutcakes
or risk heaven with three more men?
I move in, put my better eye to the glass.
Up close, the yellowed paper shows its tooth,
the story collapses to a scatter of deep scratches.
The museum guard clears his throat.
I back away, guilty. At that,

the nameless printmaker tips his hand:
He's angry at his dulled burins, the less-
than-pliant piece of wood, his failure
to get on in the pious workshop. He lengthens
a crooked cut between her eyebrows. She grows
stubborn now, not bitter. Makes her choice:
refuses rapture, putti, angels' song,
the heavens breaking open all around us.
She grits her mismatched teeth. And lives.

In Which I Forgive My Mother Her Intentions

Our father who art in heaven hallowed be thy name
thy kingdom come thy will be done on earth
as it is in heaven give us this day our daily bread
and forgive us our debts as we forgive our debtors lead
us not into temptation but deliver us from evil
for thine is the kingdom the power and the glory forever amen

For two thousand years, folks have been saying amen
to that, repeating the lives and the names
of the saints as orthodox charms to stave off the evil
that seems to swell out of every gritty lump of real earth.
My family's no exception, but in the way gold is teased out of lead
by the philosopher's stone, my mother baked bread

that could rub the pain off a wet November day, a yeast bread
we'd wait hours for, watching it rise the way we hoped a man
would one day rise out of the crowd and lead
us away from all this. We'd drop our names
to take on his. By that one meek sacrifice, we'd inherit the earth,
mount up on wings like eagles, and with his help control the evil

born in our woman-flesh. Three daughters in one house. More evil
than one father and mother could handle and still get the daily bread
on the table. Three sisters—the Fates, the Triune Goddess (earth-
underworld-sky), the virgin-mother-crone trinity. Amen,
we'd snicker, to whatever witch-hint whispered the name
we knew in secret, the hidden life we'd none of us lead

openly. *Flesh will lead*
you astray, our father assured us: *The evil*
flesh is heir to assumes many names—
greed, carnality, sloth. Our mother agreed. But it was bread
she'd turn our idle hands to, her mother's recipe, her grandmother's, a man-
catching spell (his heart, through his stomach). It called for things of earth:

butter, cakes of yeast, fresh-milled grain that even smelled of earth—
oats, barley, wheat, sometimes rye when the mood took her. She'd lead
our squeamish hands through the sticky first steps, the kneading. *A man's
hands would be too heavy,* she'd say, laying damp cheesecloth like a veil
over the deep crock bowl. The firm little knot of bread
dough hunkered in the curve like an egg. Hours later, she'd call our names—

the bowl rim would bulge over with honeycomb bread dough. Miracle of earth,
not heaven. My mother meant to lead us toward my father's god, away from evil.
But her recipes bore the names of too many mothers,
　　her womb, too many daughters. We praise her. Amen.

Preacher's Daughter

| i |

What's worse, she's forgotten
how to pay attention.
Old King James thumps along
to Judah's soldier-boy march,
and she hears footfalls
in the dust beside the parade.

Old Testament rhetoric cracks
out of Sinai, echoes off tablets
of black granite. Ever obedient,
she strains to understand,
but she's distracted by a mild chatter
above the washing stones in the river.

Soup for rangy teenage sons
bubbles in clay pots. The evensong
of weavers. Light fails.
Children drop off to sleep.
A soft pattern of threads
spreads under playing fingers.

| ii |

In the beginning was the Word
The Word was never spoken

But other words were spoken about the Word, and these spoken Words
were repeated and remembered and repeated again and became better
with the retelling, and became so good that writing was invented and
they were written down, and because these written words carried
some measure of assurance, they were copied, and then copied
again, and passed around, and then they were collected and then
they were redacted, and codified and edited and translated, and
used for selfish purposes and used for singing babies to sleep,

and then exegesis was devised to be performed on them, and then they were translated some more, and at last the printing press was invented for them and they were printed, and published, and marketed in every way marketing departments of publishing houses could concoct, and they were bound in different colors and illustrated and put to music, and great arguments were waged over every little jot and tittle, and brother turned against brother while sister turned her face away, and still the copying and the translating and the printing and the reprinting and the arguments went on

but the Word
was never
spoken

| iii |

In the way that limestone erodes
into the sea, leaving behind
a bare granite headland
to be named and charted, haunted
by mermaids who sing to sailors,
Come close, Come too close,

so we speak words
in answer to other words.

| iv |

Miriam's role was to round up the slaves.
They balked and moaned. Bondage was OK,
they'd say, if you play your cards right.
The order is set, they'd whine, caste decreed
in the stars. How else to appease the great river,
how else to petition for its overflow and fall?

The past is done, she'd slap that tambourine.
Horse and rider, whack it again,
Cast in the sea.

Moses thought he deserved a splashier exit.
Wanted some Emmy-class special effects.
This delta mudsplatter on his shins
and dirty bathrobe and sandals,
small reward for facing down a Pharaoh.

Horse and rider,
Miriam sang.
Cast in the sea.

The Pharaoh's daughter begged him to stay.
All things return, Batya hummed,
glittering lapis and gold, sandalwood
to woo a lost baby: coil and recoil.
This bumpkin god of the desert does not see.

But leave he did, left inlaid flail and chariot
and the chance to be god-king Osiris himself.
Walked away, plague and mayhem bursting
out on every side. Miriam got a few families
to follow, the poorest, who could carry
all they owned on their backs.

And ahead of them, on the far shore,
timbrel flashing, she danced
to call them over. *Horse and rider.*
Oldest couplet in scripture. *Cast in the sea.*

When the dirty rabble faced into the desert,
the youngest children heard a sound

their parents couldn't name: Time,
that seamless Egyptian circle, squalled
on a brand-new hinge never wrung before.
Swung open like a great round door,

and something—maybe it was just them—
moved forward! It did! Moved forward!
  And the history of the world
    quit going around in circles, and
      began.

| v |

What's worse, she's forgotten how to read.
The holy letters wobble, then scramble
to spell words she mustn't ever say.
At the piano, she flubs the hymns.
Overtones of unintended pitch hum
from chance nodes on the strings,

unnerving little tunes, in minor keys.
In her dreams, water drips chilly
in the dissolving throats of deep caves.
She sleeps afraid. They were there,
insists the cool water in the caves:
those ghosts you see, a limestone mold
for magma that fills anything it can.
White soft stone that bears the heat
till the fierce basalt gains its form,
the granite hidden always in its nature.
Washing away then, singing again,
a dance of ions faster and faster,

into the sea in a froth of departure,
the splash and fall of another birth.

Contralto Recitative with Angel Chorus

And there were in the same country shepherds
abiding in the fields keeping watch over
their flocks by night. And lo, the angel
of the lord came upon them, and the glory
of the lord shone round
about them. And they were sore afraid.

Their reaction's perfect. Of course they were *afraid.*
They weren't WAITING FOR THE RAPTURE, those shepherds,
as a bumper sticker I've seen around
town seems to recommend over
ordinary driving. It was dark. They were cold. The glory
shot off like fireworks, an angel

choir tuning up on an *oo-oo-oo,* the recitative angel
doing arpeggio warm-ups in a throaty contralto, afraid
she'd muff the sforzandos, her main chance for glory,
and miffed, too—you know prima donnas—that unwashed shepherds
made up the audience. "Homemade wooden flutes," she la-la'd over
the 5-tone folk scale, "and dog-whistle contests around

the campfire." "*Fart* contests," sniggered a counter-tenor, round
face spotty as a boy's. Somehow, these aren't the same angels
I used to hear about in Sunday School, over and over.
They're like any semi-pro pick-up chorus—newcomers afraid,
dumb sopranos, conductor thinks he's god. But the shepherds,
like any audience, missed all that. The fugue knit glory-halleluiahs,

the contralto's "Fear not" boomed off shale outcroppings in a glory
of echoes. She managed to control her vibrato around
the F#—it'd sounded like a Chrysler starting—forgave the shepherds
and sang like this was Handel's debut before George II. The angel
baritone section got their *pp* entrance, the disaster they were afraid
of after dress rehearsal didn't strike. When the performance was over,

they were all stunned. They'd forgotten silly costumes, wings over
church-choir robes, tinsel-glued-to-taffeta for artificial glow,
the tenor's joke about dangling from a sky hook, so afraid
they'd look more like Peter Pans and Tinkerbells flying around
than a multitude of the heavenly angel
hosts. From the downbeat, the music kindled itself. The shepherds,

bless their tone-deaf shepherd hearts, knew it. Now that it's over—
not just the song but the age of angels—the sky's quiet, all the glory
departed. Even so, when I look at the round mute moon,
                    I'm still afraid, sore afraid.

The Holy Ghost Develops Binge/Purge Syndrome

The Holy Ghost eats salt,
shoves it into His flaccid mouth
by the fistful, knuckles first, with
the unfocussed grip of a one-year-old.
He's drawn to salt—it lacks color,
as He does, it dissolves and disappears.

He gulps the humble crystal rubble
with a lurch of slackspirit Adam's apple.
It's substance He covets: gristle, cuticle,
an anchor point for the Triangle.
Some scars, a stone bruise, even a stye
might peg this sagging mystery.

He tries to deny the thirst that comes later,
the state-change, sucking the heat out of Him,
fingers swelling into almost visible cloud trails,
the shame He feels when the vapor condenses
—breath against a cold mirror—
and falls away from Him out of the sky.

The Holy Ghost Attends Vacation Bible School

The least likely place the Holy Ghost ever descended
was in east Mississippi. Red clay hills
and church politics soured on years of inbreeding.
Every deacon drove a pickup. At Bible School,
the kids played red rover and rolled down
the sharp slope behind the Baptist church.
He recognized the dizziness at the bottom
and the fear of having your name called,
but the grass stains, the torn blouses
and sprained wrists—these were beyond Him.

In the blackberry patch behind the Education Building,
He shared the children's horror of snake spit,
but the stickers that would fester in their palms
held no snag for Him—reminded Him, in fact,
of the thorns, one of The Son's biggest coups.
His envy would flare up, full flame. To boost
His self-esteem, He whispered aloud His old names:
Comforter, Paraclete. When they passed around
the red Kool-Aid and the store-bought oatmeal cookies,
the wax-paper cup that was poured for Him
spilled against the hard ground and soaked
into the sandy bare spot real feet had worn
in the clover and St. Augustine of the church yard.

The Holy Ghost Tries Out for Little League

The outfield—a position made for him!
When Lefty Gomez credited his success
to a "fast outfield," the Holy Ghost
thought He'd heard "vast," and He imagined
that field could match His spaciousness,
His inability to touch base, to stay within lines.

The high pop fly rising toward Him
kindled his old longing for the laws of motion
—that pull toward an object He could never know.
It floated out, patient as planets,
amber and gold in the late afternoon sun,
the crack of ash coming slower than the ball.

He saw two earths, wrapping their separate flights
in sweeping lines of gravity, and then
the little leather baseball plummeted
right through Him—grapeshot through flame—
and thumped in the way of all real things
against the grass near the fence.

The Holy Ghost Moves to Kilgore

After five years in the red dirt hills
of east Mississippi, the Holy Ghost moved to Texas.
East Texas. Pine trees, oil derricks, and roses.
He picked up that awful accent hard in the *r's*
and clenched in the jaw—he always was good
with languages—but He couldn't quite materialize
the skin: gritty skin that ages early, crinkles
in tiny rectangles above a starched collar line.
It's Irish, maybe Scot. Suited to damp mists
and overcast winters, too prone to fever blisters
for the Sun Belt. There was brown skin around
to inhabit, He knew, but given his theological bias,
the Holy Ghost took to the folks in charge.

He got obsessed with that white skin
—the broken cuticles, the freckles—
and once He saw a burn healing in stiff scales
across the back of a middle-aged, veiny hand
and got downright sorry for Himself.
He felt cheated. Where once He'd been so proud.
Immaterial! Invisible! Indwelling!
What good was all that now? He mused sourly,
when He'd got less purchase here than Black Spot,
than fire ants hilling on the hot medians.
The dry breeze off the rose fields reminded Him
of attar that once invoked his presence, vials
of great price broken for Him. But no body
to break for anyone. Not even disembodied.
Never any body at all.

Church Schism

Every Body's Got to Be Some Place

The Holy Ghost got caught in the middle
in a church split. He'd descended sensibly
for once, into a group with a history
of polity, but even there, a handful of Elders
decided they didn't like the preacher. At first
they didn't know why, then they prayed together
and got up a list: He was too tall, he didn't
feed them spiritually, he was awkward
with the children in the church, and one claimed
to have theological problems with his sermons
but wouldn't specify what they were.

The Holy Ghost adored lists, and felt right
at home with vagueness and Jesuitical backbite.
Whispered generalizations were His forte,
after all. But *tall!* He'd liked the guy
for being tall. For having crooked hands
to show off at the benediction. The Holy Ghost
used to pretend He had those drawn-up hands,
that faint tall-man's stoop in the upper spine,
the genial forehead wrinkles, cold sweat
on the skinny chest under the vestments.

Suckered in by Presbyterians, and see
where it got him! He felt his whole nature
had been turned against Him, those things
He liked disliked by the people He joined.
Never any place for Him—
self-pity another of His long suits—
never any place at all.

Four-Year-Old Invents a New Curse Word

After Emily Cullen emphatically said "Godshit," her parents
and their friends appropriated it as party conversation.

Michael said
God would have to shit emeralds and pure light. We said
Only a Catholic would ever say that. He said
Well then what would all you Sou-thrun Babtis's say God shits? We said
Blood! Thunder! Spears! He said
We might be getting somewhere. What, do you suppose,
the Presbyterian god would shit? We guessed
Bulwarks, canned English peas, committee schedules. He said
Not as good. What about the old Hebrew god? We yelled
Iron chariots of the Philistines, whirlwinds, fire, fire,
rams' heads, gas vans, Elijah's mantle,
bulrushes! Oh stop, he said:
What are some other gods? Someone said
The god at the freshman convocation today. What did it shit? We said
That one's a He, too. Treaties, blue blazers, manifest destiny,
tobacco ash, triangle sandwiches. Pretty good, Michael said
taking over again: What about the science god? We answered
quick on that one: Puberty, neutrons, worm gears, fugues,
Tang, skin donated for transplants, software. He said
You're mixing up the science god with the engineering god. We said
Ethics, space capsules, coffee, PVC hoses, square-root signs. He said
Different from the computer god? We said
Little electronic beeps, *this* one's an It, iClouds, roach parts,
a string with glitches, light machine oil, paprika. He said
Wow. And thought a minute and said
How about a god that's female? The women said, It's about time!
Korean orphans, rhizomes for swamp iris, leafmould, dogs' eyes
red in the dark, amaretto drinks, pomegranates. Michael said
We need a black god in here, as long as we're doing tokens. We said
You racist. He kept on
Jesse Jackson's god, the black reverend's god? We said
Undertakers, quilts, sin's breakers dashing, brimstone,
great altos, fried okra. Are you satisfied? He said

Your own, you're so sure of yourself. What does your own god shit?
Rotting father flesh, bigamy, wet tea, a run-over owl,
    ginger root, burning children, memory.
There was a pause of about two beats.
He said, Who shits bricks? None of these gods shits bricks?
We said, Sara's mother would if she were still awake.

for Michael and Sara Dunne

The Holy Ghost Designs the Perfect Woman

When The Holy Ghost first thought of making a woman,
He'd have rubbed His hands together if He'd had any.
A woman! That would show The Son, so smug
in His historic manifestation, spoiled rotten
by His status as favorite child. The one thing
on earth The Father failed to give Him.

The problem was, The Holy Ghost had always preferred men.
Men at least seemed halfway between matter and spirit.
It gave them a kind of Gnostic edge, in His opinion.
It baffled Him the way men spent as much time
yearning after women as they spent yearning
after pure idea. Women seemed to Him as soaked
with matter as a forked log sunk in a slow, warm river.

He sneered at the old stories, the sky gods who fell
on mortal women—Zeus on Europa, to cite an example.
Out-moded gods, with too many characteristics
and far too prone to hierophany.

And everyone knew The Father mixed it up
with one. Called it a one-time fling, nothing serious.
The Holy Ghost felt His scorn mounting,
His resolve waver. The Virgin Mary disgusted Him—
not merely out of family taboo, but all that talk
about baths and purification, and drips of breast milk
that transubstantiated into diamonds.

To renew His intention, He focused on AGAPE,
and in His cycling reason, a strategy formed.
He'd make her out of Himself! Make her cleanly
as argument spawns counterargument. Ribless,
as He was. Moreover, this could not diminish Him,
since any part of infinity is itself infinite. She'd be

a Holy Ghostess, beyond the grasp of any sculptor,
arriving without all the foam and scallop shells.
A masterstroke cross between Sappho and Sophia.
Fire without hearth, nurture without breast,
more eyeless than justice, more disembodied than truth.

Already boundless, He felt himself expand anew,
in love without falling, without head or heels.
A mirror vision, freed from glass or silver backing,
to worship, to adore, forever and ever. A woman
every body would want, but no body could have.
Only Him. Alone. Him alone.

WHY THE GROUNDHOG FEARS HER SHADOW

. . . Don't say it's the beautiful
I praise. I praise the human,
gutted and rising.

—KATIE FORD

God will stop at nothing
to get your heart.

—ST. AUGUSTINE

Changing Weather Patterns

El Niño slips across latitudes, rises dripping from the ocean
From seafloor mud, El Niño brings up the secrets of childhood
El Niño crawls in the manger, time runs out
El Niño rocks himself dry on the edge of a continent
Prairies of wheat go unpollinated, there is rumor
El Niño is killing the honeybees

The water turns cold, La Niña follows her twin
Windowpanes darken, the weather channel shows us rain
Angels proclaim in vain above unseasonal cloud cover
La Niña lines up her hurricanes in alphabetical order
Floodwaters announce her coming   The rich bribe airlines
while the poor push children into branches of trees

The Niños hear their names on the news in every language
The Niños bankrupt famous cities with mudslides
Comets snuff out in dirty skies   Celebrities seduce us
away from the guides in our dreams   Lovers of chaos,
computers roll back zero eyes   The trumpet cries
Los Niños in a loud voice   Faces on billboards draw closer

La Niña, we pray, *and El Niño, her brother*
We long for sweetness and scale
Our tables sag under piles of unsorted papers
Spare us, Niños   We don't know winter from summer
Above the trade winds, ozone crackles
their answer: *We have come for the children*

Shining

I am the light, standing in the kitchen window.
I do not stream or pour. I do not speak.
I repeat: I stand.

I am the light that leans down across the sink.
The kitchen sink is always there,
chanting, *everything, everything.*
I outline the man and the two little girls.
There is something about a refrigerator.
The man says the word *tattler.*
I will stand. I have all day.

I am the light that colors the hair
of the two little girls—
one head brown as wild honey,
the other white and straight
as the breath of the dying.
Brown curls is talking fast and moving her hands.
She is afraid. I stand beside her.
She is seven years old.

I am the light that shows the man punch Brown hair
in the stomach with two thick fingers.
I am the sparks that shake from the curls.
On the floor beside the sink,
I make her legs bright. They do not kick.
I show the man push Blond hair toward the dark stairs.
She is crying. The heavy fingers prod
into her back to make her hurry.
As he descends, the man dims to the sable velvet color
that hums behind eyelids.

I am the light in that squat monster, the furnace.
    I do not flicker over the coals—
    I stand, pure as taper.
    From the damp walls, flakes of peridot
    eye the grate in the furnace door.
    The Blond one has stopped crying.
    She is four years old.

I am standing in the humid basement,
    even where the man thinks it is dark enough
    to crush Blond hair, even when he makes his heart
    dense and hopeless as a dead star.
    I do not come only from the sky.
    Even here, I lift the fine blond hair.

Do not misunderstand me: I am the same light.
The man could not separate the little girls
    as he cannot separate me from my sister,
    the dark, and soon
    she will come forward with his name.

for Carroll Fisher

The Center Cannot

| i |

if I started with a different animal
and the book filled up faster than theirs
if I warmed my hands on my sister's cup
if a heartbeat sounded in the ear pressed to the pillow
if we all decided to
if we could only agree for once
if I started with another color

| ii |

if the house next door up the hill had not been locked
if the parents had not taken the same short cut
if all three sisters had still been awake
if the girls at the slumber party had not squealed
at exactly that moment
if someone had taken it in hand

| iii |

a different animal, that's what
the dream said, not color,
not start with another color,
start with a different animal

| iv |

this page seems different
I think it's a slightly different color
I'm starting a page that's another color

| v |

a different pen, if I started with a different pen
and the telephone rang in the bedroom
and the coffee was not still hot

| vi |

if I had started with a different baby
if the other baby had not cried
if the other baby had wanted what was in the refrigerator
if the kitchen had not been so far from the car
if the car had not been longer than the space in the garage
if the baby had had a better car seat
if I'd started the car with a different key
if I had a different start

| vii |

and when the sides of the photograph were cut off
and the shapes collapsed inside each other
and dimmed to neutral,

who was it who said
that if only the father
had not kept them
all in fear?

She Begins with the Sky

An infant—on her back
for so long—makes the sky
into a ground for all

subsequent gestures. Streaked, clawed,
engraved, scumbled, scraped—glyphs
of distress invented by all

resilient babies, who never
—no matter what they claim—
expunge the sky.

The Child Born

with a caul
the child who eats the skin that forms on scalded milk
the child who bites cuticles instead of fingernails
the child who sucks her hair at night
the child who sings in her sleep
the child who does not mind the squeak of blackboard chalk
the child who swallowed a blue bead
the child who will not throw up
the child who refuses to listen
the child with the gristle knob at the arch of her ribs
the child who knows where the matches are
the child who looks too long at her father
the child who likes to spit
the child who looks in the eyes of the dog
the child who sits for hours
the child who sometimes laughs when she's by herself
the child whose cold hands
the child who eats clay
the child who can look cross-eyed
the child who starts fires
the child who hides in a chinaberry tree
the child who listens
the child who grows quieter and quieter
the child who can be trusted with knives and scissors
the child who never reaches under her bed
the child who goes where no one is
the child who cuts things out
the child who hums little songs no one can recognize

The Dream Runs On

Her mother is there—don't you love mothers
in dreams!—and the new grey Ford Thunderbird
she's so proud of. A pick-up truck with 2 good ol' boys
backs up slowly into her stomach, the rusty bumper
pushing in almost to her spine. She's pinned
to the front of her own car, she can't slide

out. Actually, at first she thinks she might slide
sideways, but then notices, when she turns in the mother's
direction, that her own car has her penned
in, boxed in from the sides, with chrome guards Thunderbirds
used to have in the '50s or '60s, so that the two bumpers,
squashing tight, make a kind of cage. The good ol' boys

disappear, just drop from the dream the way men and boys
always seem to be gone when you need them. A sly dream—
the Dreamer smiles at herself, this being a bumper
year for dreams. There's only her mother
to help now, maybe she could put the T-bird
in reverse and back up. But it's so dangerous to depend

on this silly woman! When she'd suspend
caution to ask for help, in the ordinary way of girls and boys,
she'd hear the background crumple into thunder, birds
take cover in ditches, her hopes slip
away into her worst fears. Her mother,
skittish nanny goat, would bump her

eldest daughter into line, before she'd bump her
own sweet head against the ram's horns. The underpinnings
of the family required the mother
train the girls to act like boys,
to cover up, learn a shadow's oblique slide
into dark corners for when the ancient Thunderbird

arose—the Shawnee legend—the shining raptor Thunderbird,
who crashed great wings for storm—Ah!—bumped
the stars aside for room, swept mountains into landslide,
hurled lightning over water, whose warring eagle claws pinned
little girls to papered walls, who changed them into boys
for g"ood by grubbing out the mother

curled inside. Where were you, Mother, while the Thunderbird
raged? and after, when the bleeding boys wrapped down their bumpy
breasts? pinned manly smiles to all three faces,
                                        taught their thoughts to slide?

Color of the Moon

Anyone can name a baby
Anyone can name the town, too, at least in theory
Anyone can name several occasions
Anyone can name the color of the moon

Who can name the last time?
Who can see it coming far enough ahead?
Who can find the marigold bed?
Who can remember the smell?

Anyone can guess what happened
Anyone could forget the next day
Anyone could hear the conviction in her voice
Anyone could see she has it all mixed up

Who could forget a thing like that?
Who can see as far as the river?
Who can try any harder than she did?
Who could leave after that? Who could stay?

No one says the same thing any longer
No one remembers the last thing they said
No one quite remembers how they got there
No one wants to be outside alone

The Heads of Old Dolls

Everybody knows the heads outlast the bodies
Everybody knows the eyes lose their parallel glass-blue gaze
Everybody knows cross-purposes
Everybody knows the King is in chains
Everybody knows roosters up in the air
Everybody knows the cross
Everybody knows a symbol of uncertain fate
Everybody knows black pig's blood incites uprising
Everybody knows red beads tied around a gourd
Everybody knows spells drawn in cornmeal and coffee grounds
Everybody knows Jesus went to Africa
Everybody knows things bound with string or rope
Everybody knows designs in the dirt in front of a tomb
Everybody knows He came here in a slave ship
Everybody knows one pale eye sunk back in its socket
Everybody knows you lose your mind in a white dress
Everybody knows that's the *only* way He came

Groundhog's Prayer of Petition

Weather
    Before our eyes
        Close

Why the Groundhog Fears Her Shadow

It's just like you, you god-besotted woman hater. To die
today, dragging off after you half the mythology of middle winter.
Groundhog's Day—when all that's left of the future's a shadow
or the lack of it. It's Candlemas. Celtic Imbolg. In Ireland, La Fheile Brid,
the Day of St. Brigid, who is, in *The Golden Bough,* "a 'heathen'
goddess of fertility, disguised in a threadbare Christian

cloak." It's also Feast of the Purification of Women, a Christian
holy day, handy annual reminder of who's dirty. Chances are, you died
to celebrate that, but maybe, deep down in your freckled genes, a heathen
grandmother stirred like a seed in mud, refused to spend one more winter
playing lady. Enough horses sweat/men perspire/women glow. Her breed
of women won't cotton to hold-your-knees-together and stay in the shadow

of your man. Knock the sun off her? No mere man casts a shadow
large enough. And enough southern-accent Christian
trinity—"PraiseFathuhSuhnAn'Hoe-leeGhost, All-men"—grisly parody of Brid,
radiant Goddess of three faces. Blasphemy, she declared. No wonder you died!
But where do you leave me, your daughter—years later at the fulcrum of winter,
my own throat and red-haired ancestors crying out for heathen

vengeance? Creeping aboveground, I cringe like the groundhog (heathen
superstition anyway, you'd say), not so much afraid of her own shadow
as terrified she'll see the quickening winter
sun as I saw it once, my Christian
father's John-the-Baptist severed head, dying
scream a long *no-o-o-o-o* across the sky. I'm bride

to too many lovers. Bride
double-bound to father/husband, Beast and Prince alike. My heathen
scarlet heart's blood thumps toward rage, rage, to gush out, die
fighting, to drag these shape-shift shadow
trysts to light. My Christian
blood, blue blood of veins and martyrs, soughs wintry

toward a drowsy surrender, toward the ice-choke secrets of winter,
the blasted kernel, family shame veiled with the eldest bride.
In two sides of the same mouth, I chew Christian
bread with sacramental wine, and heathen
wedding feasts of meade, venison. I swallow hard. A shadow
falls across the table—my own, the outline curling in to die.

This time, sun-struck, light-blind, she stays aboveground. Dying winter
gathers its last storm. Is it her shadow summons the cold, or the bride
tearing away her veil? Purple heathen lips, eyes pale and old as Christ.

How Two Became One Again

Sestina's Work Done

This is how she came to know it, the turning
of the lines and the spell of the numbers.
The anagram in the name never occurred
to her at all. Formal rules—repeating six words
sex/woman/sin/enough/heart/voice seven times
each—snatched the narrative out of her hands

and wheeled her away. The scars on her hands
thrum, *It's my fault: I forced the door marked NO, turned*
the iron key long as a carving knife. How many times
is a child told, *Look at this*? Who keeps numbers
on such charming commands? How often do those words
imply a twin phrase, *Not at that*? It never occurred

to her to disobey, and soon half a universe never occurred,
slipped out the door one event after another, holding hands
with the homeless twin, a dirty child who was never taught words.
From then on, there were two. One who turned
smiling to Mama, source of alphabet, songs, numbers,
nursery books in blue/yellow/gold, source of good times

approved for memory. Another who waited for the bad times,
grew sullen, hoarded the events which never occurred,
invented a language of stutters and widened eyes, a number system
based on lost teeth, a broken chair, nutshells. Your father's hands
disappear behind his back, and when it's your turn
to choose, you point: One fist reappears, he speaks no words.

The fingers open: It's empty. If this game had words,
what would they be? How many times
does the smiling child choose, before her luck turns?
What if the mother is right, and none of it ever occurred?
What if the day she burned the smiling child's hands,
she put out the eyes of the twin who watched? The numbers

count backwards, sleep is on the way. Who remembers the number
she got to, before she started back down? Six/I want/five—her words
grow faint—four/three/I didn't want/two. Hands
that tried to shove the mask away sag open in sleep. Time
suspends. Scalpel does its work—clitoris, memory. It never occurred,
the mother is right again, she's waiting the daughter's return.

But, *Look at this!* The surgery turned out wrong. The numbers
reverse again, No/Yes. Whatever never occurred babbles into words.
The twins are reattached. This time: one child, two eyes, two hands.

Winter's End

What falls from the sky,
sinks. Whatever stands
has burrowed up from underground.

Staying at the Willard

$500-a-night Washington hotel,
a video history of itself on Channel 11
in every room, the lobby the place
that gave us the verb, and room service
sends up anything, even chamomile tea—
Yes Ma'am, that's 803, I think?—

and why do I feel like I don't belong here?
like I'm tricking somebody? or planning
to walk my bill? that they snicker behind
their white gloves in the famous lobby
when I walk through to the elevator, or when
they take away the teapot and squeezed bags?

It gets worse at night
when we drive back along L:
Young women dressed up like 6 year olds
playing rock star—especially the one
in the thigh-high silver pirate boots
and the blond thick long hair—

and I ask Molly and Buck if it's real hair
or a "fall" as it used to be called,
maybe still is, and did you take it off
before you went to bed?—please
don't laugh, you'll make me too sad—

and Molly thought hookers mostly did things
with the mouth—she'd just seen a movie—
and you could leave your hair on for that,
and then I had the same question
about the scarlet lipstick. This is not
a simple good/evil poem.

Molly asks Buck what happens next,
but he's got no experience with hookers at all,
so the three of us make do with what we see,
driving slow but not so slow they think
we want to talk. Back in the room, Buck said
he heard her ask, at the open window of a car,

Can I get in?
And that lets me touch the terror—to lean into
one dark car window after another and say,
Can I get in?
—I who am more than twice her age
and I who quail at dialing room service, and

I who watched, a chilly night some years ago,
the window of my own memory roll down and
swallowed once and asked the faceless shape
inside, *Can I get in?*
And I know from what happened next
she and I have the same father, the same uncle—

suit and tie when the heavy sun lies flat
against the columns of the Treasury Department
and the white satisfied curve of the south portico
and the pavements of the famous old street grid,
circles overlaying squares—and I know now when
sun and tie and suit and fine design are gone

and we've put on our ruffled baby-doll pajamas
and said our prayers and gone to sleep,
that he slips in her room and mine
—our mother drunk or dead or playing blind—
and I know now he doesn't even ask,
Can I get in? Doesn't even ask.

That blows the cover
on the pricy-hotel-guest disguise. I'm really out
there in the dark, where cars—like sheep
we're told to count—cruise by slower
than a high-heel stroll. And when I meet the one
that brakes for me—I knew exactly how to dress—

and lean in to ask, I'll know the driver's face, too,
lit green from digitals on the dashboard.
And when he hears the question
whisper damp and ticklish at his ear
from a pretty child too close to the street,
he'll give the ancient answer: *yes.*

for Molly Crouch Anderson and Buck Downs

Parish Courthouse, Cameron

Cameron's only two blocks wide,
salt water and shrimp boats
on one side, and on the other,
marsh—grass and water equal to the humid sky.
White cement WPA courthouse pokes up

through the chenier like the blunt tip of a thumb.
In front, live oaks reach heavy over the sidewalk.
Bronze plaques weigh against their roots, veterans,
long lists—Fontenot, Duhon, Theriot, Savoie,
generations of them. We meet Sheila

a block down shore at the visitors center. Shell art
for sale, postcards of pelicans, bleached skulls
of gafftop catfish that form "a natural cross"
with a miraculous rattle—she shakes one
for us—Roman soldiers casting dice, casting dice still.

Sheila has always lived here, she tells us,
worked down at the courthouse eight years,
could tell us stories, *cher.* Without segue, she says
she believes sexual molestation of children
is higher here than anywhere. I do not say this:

I believe Betty and I together could pull this topic
out of a concrete wall without our saying a word.
At least Sheila believes there's somewhere better,
on this one score. That somewhere there's a place
crazy old men do not grab and fondle twelve year olds.

Or at least if they do, the mother doesn't tell her
not to speak of it. Or at least if she doesn't, the High Sheriff
in the courthouse doesn't say, "There's nothing I can do,"
or at least if he does, the child's friends are not forbidden
to see her anymore by their parents, or at least if they are,

the child grows up and meets someone years later
she can drive across south Louisiana with,
                and see the sights.

for Betty

Woman in the Middle

Forgiveness of the father comes deep, announces in the bowels.
The sacrum, the lower chakras relax years of resentment at once,
with no warning at all from the proud mind or blindsided heart.
Trumpet eight-beat F#—son's breath, sound like fine paper tearing—

unlatched the lower spine, those oldest caches of resentment.
I don't want to let this go, to open to this, even in a poem,
even on paper. Downbeat. My son's long trumpet note tore into me,
I went dizzy, aghast, no blood for my face, there was a stink.

Didn't want to let go, to miss the music, the evening. No poem
would choose to mention food poisoning. I stumbled out. Strangers
saw my bloodless ghastly face—I was dizzy, there was that stink—
they hauled me to the public bathroom. Completely on its own

the body chose food poisoning, stumbled on this strange unmentionable
to announce that bygones had released the future. The generation turned.
A woman between two men, rushed from recital hall to bathroom,
reminded: All fears, shames, loves, are finally in the body, and finally public.

THE CASTLE OF EITHER/OR

a fairy tale

God comes to you disguised as your life.

—PAULA D'ARCY

The Castle of Either/Or

Once upon a time, there was a family that lived a long way from anyone else. At first, there had been a grandmother, but she was dead. There were two fathers, a good father who played with the little children and made sure they got enough to eat, and a wicked father who hit them. The wicked father kept the first daughter in his bed to keep him warm. The mother was blind and sat by the hearth and sang songs. A secret hid in the first daughter's hand. She kept her hand closed.

One winter, deep snow piled to the tops of the doors, and no one could leave the house. The family ran out of food. The good father heard the hungry children cry. He pushed his way out through the snowdrifts to look for food, and they never saw him again. When the wicked father heard the hungry children crying, he was very angry. He ate the little children, one by one. He did not eat the first daughter because he kept her in his bed to keep him warm. The mother sat by the cold hearth and sang. Two secrets hid in the first daughter's hand.

The winter grew deathly cold, and all the wood was gone. A stick at a time, the wicked father burned the house. He burned the floor, then the roof, and finally the walls. He kept the first daughter in his bed to keep him warm. When the hearth was gone, the blind mother sang one last song, and died. Three secrets hid in the first daughter's hand. She kept her hand closed.

The last stick of the house burned away, the father died, snow melted, and winter was over. The first daughter walked out into the world. She had nothing to take with her but three secrets. The first secret was a ring from her grandmother, too small to fit on anyone's finger. When she turned the ring against her palm, it chanted:

Woeful plight, Woeful plight.
Stop your ears and quench your sight.
Where is here? Here is where?
Blink, my child. Leave here for there.

The second secret was a pebble from her little sister. When the first daughter squeezed the pebble, it grew warm and bestowed courage. The third secret was a bowl from her mother, too small to hold even a crumb. When the girl turned the bowl upside down, she heard her mother's songs.

First daughter loved the beautiful world outside the family house. She picked violets and clover blossoms, gathered wild berries and nuts to eat, and laughed as she watched the silly squirrels. When sunset came, evergreen needles and dry leaves made a bed. If the leaves scratched her arms and kept her awake, the ring chanted, she blinked, and forgot where she was. When night was cold, the pebble kept her warm. And every night, the bowl sang her to sleep.

She wandered for a long time. Terrifying adventures came her way, but the pebble gave her courage. There were great distances to walk. When she thought she could go no further, she turned the ring:

Where is here? Here is where?
Blink, my child. Leave here for there.

And she blinked, forgot her tired feet and continued along the road.

A troll posed an impossible test, but the bowl sang this little song :

Noon and midnight, laughter/tears.
Brighten eyes, perk up your ears.
You will end this woeful plight.
Spiral, spiral, then turn right.

And she obeyed the song's words and passed the test.

One day, she came to a castle. The castle was built of gray stone blocks hewn straight, with heavy iron doors and words carved above them:

Far is near and near is far
Either/Or, Either/Or

She read the words aloud. Slowly, the iron doors swung open. She squeezed the pebble, walked inside, and called out. The castle was silent.

She found one empty room after another, all made of grey stone blocks hewn straight. At length, she came upon a pair of tall wooden doors. She remembered the words from the castle door, and spoke them aloud:

Far is near and near is far
Either/Or, Either/Or

Slowly, the wooden doors swung open, and she walked inside. High windows lit an enormous hall. She saw no one. The hall was silent.

A wide tapestry lay in front of her on the stone floor, many steps across and many steps long. Woven into the tapestry were animals she had never seen before, in strangely shifting colors. The animals moved about. Green vines crept in every direction. She stood a while at the edge of the tapestry, and then took a step. The animals moved away from her footstep, and the vines curled back. The hall was silent. She was afraid to go on. The ring turned in her palm, and chanted:

Where is here? Here is where?
Blink, my child. Leave here for there.

The girl blinked and forgot where she was. In front of her, the animals opened a path, and she took step after step.

After a while, the path closed. She looked up. She turned all the way around to see what was in the hall, but she saw nothing but walls made of gray stone blocks hewn straight. A loud voice spoke: *Welcome to the Castle of Either/Or.* The words were so loud they set up echoes:

Eagle/sparrow? Bird or beast?
Which the hunger? Which the feast?
Poisoned honey? Peace or war?
Either/Or, Either/Or.

The ring turned by itself, and turned again. The ring's chant was drowned out by the echoes, and the girl did not blink. She waited. The pebble warmed. *Tell me what to do,* she said. The echoes set up again:

Either/Or. Either/Or.
You have come from near or far.
Slave or Princess. Win or lose.
In the castle, you must choose.

When the echoes died down, the voice whispered: *First Daughter, you have come all this way to decide between the good father and the wicked father.* There were no echoes.

She looked left and right and did not know what to do. The ring turned and turned against her palm, but the girl's eyes opened wide and she refused to blink. The bowl turned upside down in her palm and hummed a little tune, but the tune had no words. The pebble was warmer, but it had no answers. At last she dropped her head and said: *I don't know.* Then the voice was impatient: *Your life will go on for a long time. Either you remember the good father and forget the wicked father. Or you remember the wicked father and never think of the good father again.* The echoes took up:

Which is better, tear or stitch?
Either/Or. Which is which?

The odd words filled the girl. Her life would go on for a long time. How could she remember only the wicked father who killed her brothers and sisters and kept her in his bed to keep him warm? How could she remember only the good father who played with her and made sure she got something to eat? The bowl did not sing. The ring was still because she refused to blink. The pebble was even warmer but did not have answers. The figures on the tapestry went on moving about, just as before.

Then she thought of the troll and posed a test. Turning the ring a quarter turn, she forgot the good father and remembered only the wicked father. A draft of cold air crossed her face. Her fist tightened around the secrets, but she refused to blink. She lowered her eyes to the tapestry right around her feet. The animals had crisp outlines and fine, bright colors. Some ran as fast as they could, looking left and right. After them galloped larger ones with pointed teeth and long sharp claws. Others joined in a wild dance, laughing and yelling. Shadows darkened beneath the green leaves of ivy. The dance moved faster and faster, and the dancers began to fall. The girl raised her eyes. The hall was silent.

She turned the ring a quarter turn the other way. She forgot the wicked father and remembered only the good father. She looked around the tapestry, and saw animals and plants in every direction, too many to count. As she looked, their outlines softened, and the colors faded. She yawned, and the animals and plants lined up into rows and circles, all the way to the edges of the tapestry. She saw that she stood at the very center. Her fist relaxed, and the ring fell and bounced away. The hall was silent.

She stood still for a long time. Then she squeezed the pebble hard and made her choice. She spoke loudly, but her voice shook: Both. I choose to remember both. There was a great rumble, and the stone blocks began to shake. The voice roared: *Selfish girl! Who are you to dare ask for everything!* The echoes shrieked: *Selfish girl. Selfish girl.* The high windows went dark. An icy wind rushed around the hall.

First daughter was terrified. The pebble burned her hand, and her fist flew open. Pebble and bowl dropped and rolled away. She covered her eyes and fell. The voice rumbled with the stone walls and howled with the wind: *You are banished from the Castle of Either/Or. No magic will go with you. You bear this curse: Your eyes will open too wide. No matter what they see, they will not look away.*

Without even an echo or puff of smoke, the Castle of Either/Or was gone. The girl's eyes opened wide, and she found herself in a world filled with people. She watched young people laughing and holding hands. She saw babies starve in cold winters, and soldiers bleed in the mud, alone. She saw an old woman stabbed and robbed, and someone come to bandage the wounds. She watched wildflowers grow out of filth. She saw many children taught to keep secrets. Her grandmother's ring was lost, but she wanted to know where she was. The bowl was lost, but she sang the songs from memory. The pebble was gone, but she found courage of her own. She made her way with her hands open. She told some people about the good father and a few about the wicked one. She never told anyone about the castle. She lived for a long, long time, but whether she lived happily or unhappily, she would never say.

DAUGHTER'S FEALTY

You've gone so far.
Maybe you've forgotten.

You've gone so far.
Maybe you've forgotten.

You've gone so far.
Maybe you've forgotten.

—HMONG SINGER POV THOJ

Continental Divide

3655 m   12,061 ft
Loveland Pass, Colorado
—NATIONAL PARK SERVICE SIGN

Yesterday we drove over the pass at Loveland.
Snow gauzed the crests. Between the peaks,
great bowls of white up-tilted
to the Colorado lacquer of the sky. Scallops
huge as meadows followed us like turning faces
as we eased up the last saddle to the pass.

And then over.
Nothing is the same.
The scallops are a lesser shade of blue,
the flash-pan sun no longer slashes at our eyes.
Our ears popped once or twice
and we yawned on the descent.

When we were children,
he brought us here.
The Great Divide,
his God voice calling up
another natural wonder:
Watershed of the Continent.

Buoyant summer—the mountain columbines
preened for their reflections in a tender sky.
The idea got us light-headed.
He stopped the car and we spit on both sides,
my mother embarrassed
before the passing cars.

One later summer, I came here with him.
My lips tugged with irony, braces, defending
my hard-won smallholding from invading sovereignty.

I looked away when he pointed, pretended
to read in the back seat, muttered,
Could you find the line without the park signs?

Yesterday, the snowfields hushed us.
Rim to rim, the sky a dry enamel blue
and him dead. We could have shed
tears that would flow in two oceans,
but the car coughed when we topped out
and we all thought: *How thin the air is
at such an altitude.*

Steam Calliope

Blue-Ribbon Float, 4th of July Parade

| i |

Strangers, tourists at the small-town parade,
wincing when we bump shoulders. We shuffle
in the bowl of a narrow mountain valley
that now—without warning—clamors
like a three-alarm bell: paddle-wheel steamboat
in the Mississippi channel? Coney Island
merry-go-round? Mill whistle gone haywire?
Cowering—fortissimo assault on all ears—we see
a sheet-metal flue heave toward us, tall as aspen,
soot black against the blue-glazed Colorado sky.
Wavering pitches shove against each other:
Bill Grogan's Goat opens our throats—
  our hearts fly into our mouths,
    our hats fly into the air—
      our hearts leave our mouths
        and fly up after our hats.

It's our favorite song.

The whistle blew. The train drew nigh:
It's the Industrial Revolution—all flying steam,
all fly-ball governors and machined caps, die-cast
worm gears, sheet copper glinting like fireworks.
Bill Grogan's goat is doomed to die.

Crazed thunderheads whiz up
  like coveys of flushed quail.
    It's an outsized whistling teakettle,
      and it's getting closer.
        It's a giant espresso machine.

It could blow up any minute.

Now we see, in striped stokers' aprons,
young men ride the float. Snap chamois cloths,
jiggle counterweights, eye the flywheel—
fine in green paint, fine disregard
for intonation. It's right in front of us,
we're jack-hammered into the pavement.
Our lungs flatten, our eyes water.
Bill Grogan's goat . . .
flags the train at last

and the diapason fades.

Deafness after detonation:
we look but can't hear, press together on the curb,
our eyes level with the knees of the stokers.
They are altar boys, functionaries. When will our sins
be forgiven and the Gloria begin? They twist
acorn nuts, tap glass pipe gauges, bleed off
pressure from a port like the spit valve on a trumpet,
in good time complete their offices, and at last,
at last, an invisible high priest wheels into—
Popeye the Sailor Man. We cheer,
we rock back and forth in relief,
pound each other on the backs.

It's our favorite song.

Pop-Eye the sailor MAN WRONG NOTE!
We flinch—a blow to all stomachs. *MAN* missed
again. *MAN* AGAIN! We are battered silly.
The stokers roll their eyes, nudge each other—
you learn at your first piano recital
not to poke around to find the right note.

And now we see the old geezer himself,
engineer's cap pushed back on his head, manning
a j-rigged keyboard of wooden levers.
He's playing by ear, showing the tip of his tongue.
Pop-Eye the Sailor Man
He is Pecos Bill, straddling the hurricane.
I'm Pop-Eye the Sailor Man
He is Orpheus, charming the elements to time signature.
I like to go swimmin' with bow-legged women
He does not know we are listening!
I'm Pop-Eye the Sailor Man.

He Is Who He Is.

Bottomless quiet—we grope for our bearings.
The stokers, bled of sound, are computer programmers,
market reps from Denver, costumed from a history
when steam drivers plumbed mineshafts for silver,
locomotives wheezed cumulus that shooed buffalo herds.
We count cylinders of the manifold—
eight brass whistles, one note each:

His repertory is limited.

Go Tell Aunt Rhody, the calliope orders
the rimmed valley. The oak-staved boiler
is moving away from us, cinching hoops
bright as army spitshine. The flue sighs
sparks against the darker mountains behind it.
Go Tell Aunt Rhodie, it wails again.
I am losing sight of it: rivets, collet chucks,
conjured storm clouds, jigsaw bearing-bronze.
An altar boy hefts a quarter log of spruce,

and at the base of the boiler chamber,
  opens the cast-iron door to the firebox.
    Go tell Aunt Rhodie, pleads the machine,
    The old grey goose is dead.

    I look straight into the fire.

| ii |

A different valley, gentler:
We moved so often,
I always had to ask my mother
which one. The steeple
of the tiny Baptist church boasted
chimes—one single octave, no black keys.

The technological imperative
came over him: he'd play
almost every night. Through trial
and much error, he figured out
a coincidence in range with the old
bagpipe hymns: *Amazing Grace,*

How Firm a Foundation.
The first line of *Joy to the World*
stumped down the eight consecutive notes
like an archangel with big news,
and he was OK till heaven and nature
tried to sing toward the end of the stanza.

My mother cooks supper in the parsonage,
my sister and I hang on her cotton skirt.
I see brush marks in the green paint
on the door fronts of the kitchen cabinets.
We're spun off our feet as she whirls around,

grip tighter to her skirt for balance,

spun to face the porch where our setter
nurses female puppies. Outside the door,
screenless in that greenish summer,
the valley trembles like a struck bell:
A Mighty Fortress Is Our God, only one
one sharp missing from the melody line.

My mother is humming along,
sawing drumstick from second joint.
Grease heats up on the little gas stove.
She smiles shyly,
  adores his flamboyance,
    cringes and blushes
      maybe still, in her grave,
        at the wrong notes.

Bass Fishing with a Hulapopper

| i |

I rouse before dawn, to look for answers
alone by the lake, but the pier holds a stick figure
already—casting. In the near dark I know
Sean by his hunched shoulders: me-against-world.
It's not a time for chat, but there are formalities:
Doin' any good? I ask. *Naw,* the obligatory answer.
The little pond lies quiet around him,
the warm water smoking mist witches.

Only what is close to me is in focus,
broken out in a fine jet-bead sweat.
Blackberry blossoms spread plain-Jane faces
for spring. Too early for fruit, bramble claws
its way down the mud bank, promise of summer,
of berry-wet mouths and hands stained magenta,
pricked with stickers sure to fester.

The waterbreath goes pastel as I walk
toward Sean at the end of the pier. We suspend
inside a freshwater pearl, inside soap bubble
colors, lost to ups and downs, distance—
an island in the Pacific. The water is shallow
as the sky, and the careful skin to separate the two
will stretch through only later, with the sun.

Sean casts for bass, I fish for words.
The same straight pine trees take off
into the fog that yellows around us.
Sean's father left him the answer,
brain-splattered across a lined legal pad:
Now that I've got your attention—
I'm dead. My answer is slower coming,

the paper I've brought with me still blank.
What is a father who does not open
to the future? A daughter
who does not quicken her father?
Father death, child failure. No words
to live by. I grasp for my stock hope:
Maybe the answer's in nature.

But I have more luck
    in Sean's tackle box
        than in mayhaw crowns
            that black the lake shores.

| ii |

Only what's close to me is in focus.
The tackle box, lying between us,
splays open in steppes, the valley
of an old river. The topmost tray
disgorges handfuls of artificial worms,
squirmy frog-flesh latex, in day-glo colors.

I lean closer, smell bug dope,
WD-40. The second tray down
offers satisfying constants in gear—
spools of monofilament/12# test,
red & white bobs, lead sinkers
I once bit with new 8-year molars.

Sean's changing his lure. Handle propped
between his feet, top guide eye bent toward his hands,
the rod's a live, nodding thing. Rising light gleams
in the next lowest tray. In tidy square compartments,
here the big lures phosphoresce, preen,
freshwater plugs—the names—

their names are coming back to me, every one—
moon-sheen pretty as eye shadow worn
too young, tinsel flakes sunk in amber varnish,
an inverse camouflage designed to attract attention.
Reddened erotic curves imply widemouth bass,
horny as the teenager at the bait shop.

The mistwitches exit offstage into the willows,
and the light rises another notch. I see
the bottom, where a good child would never reach
her hand. Bead eyes catch mine, the lean flanks
of a crankbait gar, hung along its underbelly
with triptych hooks enough to snag an entire shoal.

Gaping back at me
from the polished chrome lip
of a deep-running lure:
            my own accusing eye.

| iii |

The eye widens, turns guilty, backs off.
I look away, smooth out the page in my lap.
Dry land is dividing from the waters.

Our shimmery soap bubble dulls, thins,
goes patchy to a tired surface tension.
Soon it will blink and scatter.

| iv |

A whistle: Sean's casting rod slices through air.
Reel plays out a long buzz. One tick of silence,
and *ploop,* the lure lands soft in the shallows.

Perfect cast. Sean lets it sit still two beats,
then with a wrist motion flicks the rod tip
backwards. Full seconds

later, at the edge of the lake, the top-water lure
jerks toward us, against the water's surface:
G# plink and a little glissando

What is it? Where am I?
Hulapopper! I didn't know they still—
past loss, past grief, past anger,

the smoldering bunch in Sean's shoulders—
I knew that reminded me of something!—
G# pitch true as the bone flute of a shaman

and daughter and father are in someone else's boat,
we were always in someone else's boat,
drowsy from getting up so early.

Dimensionless spherical light pillows us
from all sides. Across the empty boat seat
between us, my father nudges toward me

a brand new bait. *Hulapopper,* he grins,
knowing I'll take to the word: *the latest thing.*
He's teasing me with it,

pretending it can speak:
Aloha. Nudge. *Aloha: Hello.*
Nudge. *Aloha: Good-bye.*

Brown tobacco,
spit on a plug for luck
and the long cast into fuzzy distance.

| v |

Fishing lure made hula dancer: close to me,
in focus. Round painted head, glassy eye
of a cornered girl-child at her father's mercy.
Red concave impossible mouth, wide
as my child-palm, scoops a tablespoon of water

forward at any tug from the leader
half-hitched to the eyelet in her throat.
Dragged through the water, her hips thrash
side to side, fringed saucy with pink-plastic
Hawaiian grass skirt. Cute—

as it all was in the early '50s. Little girls
made of double-refined sugar and cinnamon,
and their daddies shine toothy
Pepsodent grins from every Kodak snapshot
to prove everything

is A-OK, the Union still adding states,
my mother is pregnant, and the world
safe for democracy.

| vi |

Sean backflicks his rod a second time.
From the edge of the lake, the hulapopper's
open mouth gurgles again her single plainsong.

Our Fathers, I translate for Sean and for me:
Our Fathers, Who turned their faces away,
Whose promises were too great,

Who died to show us what fools we are
to be taken in, Who drew us up
out of our safety and formlessness

at the muddy lake bottom, snagged us
with hooks enough for a thousand children.
You died! Without a backward glance!

and we're left to flop in the gritty aluminum hull
of a borrowed boat, gills muscling for oxygen,
frightened eye clouding over.

Sean's third tug of the rod.
Her obedient mouth *gulps* a panpipe pitch
that unlocks the curled fingers

of a death clutch. My father turns.
His fist opens like a simple flower, promise
of mouths wet with juice the color of blood,

angry scratches from the briar canes
and the hot Missouri sun, long Saturdays
when we never caught a thing,

ate blackberries and oily sardines
in a boat rocking us both
on the lap of a calm lake.

| vii |

Sean flicks the rod a last time.
The motif sounds. Still no strike,
no early morning bass.
The safety clicks, well-oiled

reel shurs a grudging reprieve:
last bobble of the little dancer,
dragged choking toward us
across the polished lake surface.

The hot sun-eye splits through
and the green and blue puzzle pieces
lock into place. Up and down
let go each other and settle out

where they belong. The acrid past
burns off behind us—mist leaving
the water—and the future tucks itself
into the nubby sepals of white vine blossoms.

Dragged toward us through wave
after wave of reflected light. Brown tobacco,
spit on a plug for luck. I rose to the bait,
every time. Still do.

Small steady ripples set up
their whispers at the edges of the pond.
Aloha, they repeat, repeat.
        Good-bye, Hello.
                Aloha. Good-bye.

for Betty Armstrong and Sean Kirby

Roundball

Sportscaster: DeWayne Scales, SEC Tournament
MVP! Great game! Great *game!*
Scales: I did. Yes, I did.
—CBS POST-GAME INTERVIEW

|i|

My father died watching
the LSU-Georgia basketball game. Watched it
on his homemade TV in Leland, my mother
fixing supper in the next room.
I was in the Assembly Center
in Baton Rouge, so in a way
you could say I was there when it happened.
My son's braces came apart in the 2nd half
when he chewed ice from his coke
—I stared in my palm where he spit
the wires and metal bands. They shone white
in TV floodlights that cast no shadow—
I saw right through my hand.

Mama said later she thought he was yelling
at the TV funny: Not "Dale Brown, you jughead!
You're askin' for a turnover. Penetrate!"
like she'd come to expect, but "Me!
Throw it here! I'm open! I'm open!"

And sure enough, when she went in to call him to eat,
the screen was showing reruns of a tarpon rodeo
in Corpus Christi, and he was the color of eggplant
from his shoulders up, head flopped between his knees,
knuckles dragging the floor beside his feet.
"When they fall like that—symmetrical— "
the mortician's fingersnap
popped like molars on buckshot:
"They never knew what hit 'em."

| ii |

The brothers could sky

—RUDY MACKLIN, AFTER LSU PLAYED ALCORN

My father distinguished himself at Louisville seminary
playing center on the basketball team.
"Big Bob Leavell" hero of his Greek class,
"Mighty rough for a preacher boy."

We'd crawl up on his lap to touch
the scar under the point of his chin, beg
for the story: Smashed
into a cinderblock wall. High school gym.
Blocked a layup, too. Broke the guard's arm
and still drew the charge.

Without sons, he taught his daughters
the box-and-one, when to go man-to-man,
how to hold for the last shot and not flinch
when you got it. We dribbled
with our eyes closed, practiced
crip shots from either side. And then grew up
to make him sorry for it. Crowed
our horny delight at his ghostly TV set
where limber black giants, smooth calves
long as our freckled arms, crashed the boards
or floated in like silk for a 360.

"The old Celtics," he'd fume. "Now *that* was basketball.
Pick and roll, precision plays, y'had Sharman,
Bob Cousy—none uh' this choke at the foul line."
We'd howl back in his face: "Character ball!
Flat-footed white boys in short socks."

He'd been tall enough to play center posting up low,
but the game grew up and left him. The names

—Olajuwon, DeWayne, Jabbar, Isiah-with-one-A—
took leave of any language he could parse.
Shoulder bulk from weight machines, Ibo heights
above 7 feet seemed to him like cheating.
When the game took to the air,
it left him on the ground. Point guards
outgrew him, no sons grew past him,
white and gangling, to restore the honor
of his game and make things
like they should have been.

| iii |

I always wanted him different than he was,
and I thought he died wrong, too. Why not
waft into the cosmos on the high-C
of a tenor aria, or take wing from a cypress tree
with a single blue heron, into a shrimp-colored dawn
above the marsh? Or even if he'd sort of mixed himself
up with Jesus and died right before Easter.

But to throw himself in front of a fast break! To wring
that cautious scrim adults draw before any
knee-wrenching arena. To fling headlong
into blast-boned contact in the paint, chest bashing
hard male chest—women *oooo*-ing
on the sidelines, nails muffed with pompoms,
lines they dare not cross stenciled right on the floor—
Nikes squealing on yellow varnish, galvanic *pank*
of ball against polished oak, *Get out the way*
old man, Cedric Henderson windmill'
in foa rock-the-baby and amino acids
unknit, sphincters gaped, swollen old diabetic
heart shrugged once and the veiny legs
didn't even kick.

| iv |

What is it that leaves? The skin falls,
a used sack. And where
does it go? The face
—I saw it—not a face at all.

Is it noise leaving a firecracker?
Light seeping from a cheap tin lantern?
Does it broadcast outward, EM waves
generated by the glowing coils of our
nerves? When the circuits break,
gear-locking grind of each cell's gasp,
does the last fleet vision of catastrophe or passion
transmit its signal at the constant speed
of light? Does it jam airwaves, rattle the ionosphere,
and—strength in inverse proportion
to distance squared—tangle into mere static
with the squawk of every other living thing
that gave up the ghost the same way?

| v |

My father could never stand to lose
himself in a crowd. When the body's containment
went patchy, he tried to piggyback the waves
already there—an old ham
radio trick to boost your skip—
fans roaring, court floor polished,
sportscasters on national hook-up,
500 lux of pure halogen, drum roll
by the Brass Band from Tigerland,
players adorned for combat in hieratic
gold, purple, the enemy satanic red.

Focussed like a double-loop transmit antenna
in the direction of the roundball
arching toward the hoop, score tied,
us all holding our breath
as the final buzzer went off.

Piggybacked the 66 MHz beam, NBC sports network
at the height of the SEC conference race,
and wailed out into some Siberia corner,
some last and farthest wisp of the exploding
universe, to crackle there with echoes
of the Big Bang, the shimmy of quasars,
faith-healer sermons from pirate radio
stations along the Mexican border.

It wasn't quite right. He never approved
of finger rolls, steroids, blacks in the game,
seven varieties of slam dunk. But in the end
it was the best shot he had
and he took it: just off the left
of the top of the key,
        right over the zone.

"My Father Will Have Two Dozen on the Halfshell"

ordering at Phil's Oyster Bar in Baton Rouge

Gulf oysters are milky, grown fat
in braising seawater. The Gulf's a warm pool,
on chuffy oil burners, a crock pot
of Guatemalan blood and Cajun spices.

My father spoke of other beds, of blind tongs
groping to a clean salt shoal: Virginia tidewater,
him fresh from the seminary, before he'd failed, asea
with a smiling deacon host in a small boat.

Under their boat, I see an oyster crunch away
from its drowned bed, snapping aloose
like pliers a dentist clamped on my deadened tooth
once, and bumped off with a careless elbow.

Sometimes they just won't open, he'd tell me,
slumped against his forearms on the metal table.
No matter how you jab at the hinge
with that stubby knife.

He'd eat them with me, at Phil's, and say *Obliged.*
But mainly he would see the open boat.
The cold Atlantic bitterness. The favor. I'd see
pearls, spilling from his mouth like a god's.

NOTES

I'm indebted to the Persian poet Jelaluddin (Rumi) for the poem on the frontispiece, "Somewhere, beyond the idea . . ." These lines are from *The Essential Rumi,* translated by Coleman Barks (New York: HarperOne, 2004); to Diane Marks for calling my attention to it in a new context; and to Misagh Naderi for illuminating for me the mystery in the grand old poet.

I'm grateful to Van Wade-Day for the painting that's used on the front cover of the book.

Thanks to Carolyn Keene, author of *The Mystery of Lilac Inn* (New York: Grosset & Dunlap, 1931), for the second epigraph for the first section, and to Clara Haymon for her research to locate it.

The first epigraph for the second section is from the poem "Song After Sadness" by Katie Ford, copyright © 2012. The second epigraph for the second section is from St. Augustine.

The epigraph to the third section is from Paula D'Arcy, expressed during her retreat talks on spirituality.

NOTES

"The Center Cannot" is indebted to W. B. Yeats for its title and to Laura Mullen for the slumber party.

"Woman in the Middle" is indebted to Vance Bourjailie, for the description of a trumpet's attack as "the sound of fine paper tearing," and to Houston Haymon and Bob Leavell for teaching me to love the sound of trumpets.

I'm indebted to Pov Thoj, Hmong singer, and his translator, Kao Kalia Yang, for the lyrics in the epigraph for the fourth section. These lines are from *Two Lines XIV: World Writing in Translation,* edited by Zack Rogow (San Francisco: Two Lines Press, 2007).

Many thanks to my poetry writing students, over many years, for their dedication to craft and for their radical and fearless honesty, and to the first poetry writing class I ever taught, at LSU in 1985, for teaching me the power of the sestina form to explore language and reveal new material.

And, as always, to Cordell